Echoes of Faith and Love

Echoes of Faith and Love

Collections of a Fallen Dove

Faith Alanna Richardson

ARPress
ILLUMINATING IDEAS
EMPOWERING VOICES

ARPress
45 Dan Road Suite 5
Canton MA 02021

Hotline:1(888) 821-0229
Fax:1(508) 545-7580

Ordering Information:
Quantity sales. Special discounts are available on quantity purchases by corporations, associations, and others. For details, contact the publisher at the address above.

Printed in the United States of America.

ISBN-13:	Paperback	979-8-89356-700-7
	eBook	979-8-89356-701-4

Library of Congress Control Number: 2024903445

TABLE OF CONTENTS

PART I

For the word, Faith, a poem 1

She Lives 2

Security 3

Rain 4

The Butterfly 5

A Chance 6

Knock Knock 7

Blue Song (For Grandma) 8

For Everything 9

Space 10

No Answer 11

Me as a Word 12

Life 13

Look Towards 14

Fallen Dove 15

Forget Me Not 16

In My Own Way 17

I Am Faith 18

PART II

The Fool 22

Footsteps of Love 23

Say Love 24

Lost in Thought 25

Heart of Glass 26

One Blue Rose 27

To Pay the Price..28

Once Again 29

Alone Again 30

Lovers Twine 31

Out of Need 32

Being Alone/Being Together 33

Sunshine...34

Only Briefly...35

The Letter...36

Silent Song 37

Woman 38

Disengage 39

Goodbye 40

To Love Again 41

January 9, 1978

"I guess one of my biggest dreams was to become a great poet, like Marie Evans, Langston Hughes, Nikki Giovanni, Gwendolyn Brooks, etc.…

I really love to write poems. Some of them are very deep and some aren't; nevertheless, they're all mine."

– Faith Alanna Richardson

For the word, Faith, a poem

It's not what's in a name, but
it's what's in a person who carries
the name!

Me!

I am bold, I am beautiful, I am great,
but most of all I am black.

Look at me and you can see
life, hope, love, togetherness,

For I represent those things.
Why do I call myself these things?

For I am everything you are not
or will be, for I am

Me!

She Lives

She lives not for life only, or for
the pleasure that life may bring her.

She lives not for existence only,
for she would exist without really trying.

She lives not for reality only,
for she is the reality.

She lives not only for love,
for she is the one who made love what it is.

Who is this person and what does she live for?
If not for all these things,
she lives for you...

Security

Lucky are the ones
who know where their life is going…

Lucky are the ones
who know what they want out of life…

Have pity for the ones
who are still trying to find who
they are and what they feel.

For they are merely alone,
without meaning,
without security,
without hope…

Rain

I like days when it is just about to rain.

There is no sun, no heavy clouds or pollution,
but a cool and gentle breeze,
as if life were being renewed.

And if you, perhaps, inhale,
you might be able to smell the fresh
aroma of rain.

As the trees sway back and forth
and the gentle breeze moves along its way,
it's a rare day like this
that makes me feel being aware
and alive
is worth the while.

The Butterfly

The Butterfly is free.
He owns no one and
no one owns him.

For he is free
and his spirit runs
wild to chase his never-
ending dreams.

The Butterfly
has to be free,
with no holds, no rules to bound him.
He must come and go as he pleases.

The Butterfly is free,
Free to search, find, and see.
He can discover, unlike
You and me…

A Chance

A chance to dream
the dream of all,

A chance to see
all that should be seen,

A chance to know
all that is never known,

A chance to be
all that we should have said,

A chance to wish
that all would go away,

A chance to change
all that we did,

A chance to live
our life over and never
the same way…

Knock Knock

Knock knock
Winter's gone and Spring's at the door.
With it comes brisk, breezy days and
happy hayrides.

Knock Knock
Spring's gone and Summer's at the door.
With it comes hot days, cool nights,
early days and late nights, bicycle rides,
slow walks, and lazy picnic
lunches.

Knock Knock
Summer's gone and Autumn's at the door.
With it comes the turning of the colors
(orange, red, yellow), raking of the leaves,
bringing in the harvest, nature going
into hibernation, and county fairs saying
their goodbyes.

Knock Knock
Autumn's gone and Winter's at the door…

Blue Song (For Grandma)

Blue Song,
who sings the song?
Who knows the tune?
Grandma can, 'cause
she named it when she was young,
while the world was upset and
trying to regain its composure.

Blue Song,
who sings the song?
Who knows the melody?
We do, 'cause
we sing it everyday of our lives,
when morning comes around and night is not yet forgotten.

We all sing the song,
Just as our Father did for us.
Life ain't changed and neither will the tune…

For Everything

For every rough, there is smooth.

For every hard, there is soft.

For every noise, there is silence.

For every fight, there is peace.

For every count, there is numbers.

For everything, there is a cause, and for every
cause, there is a reason, and for the reason
I have sought nothing, but to be still,
be neutral,
be lifeless,
be of no pertinence
except to be there alone…

Space

As I lean forward,
I long to be caught.

For if I fall, I will fall into
an empty darkness with no place of
value at all.

Just space that seems to go on
forever…

No Answer

When you're all alone,
who gives you an answer
for your questions?

What goes through your mind?
What do you say?

Be very still and listen carefully.
What do you hear?

A clock that ticks away, a truck, a car, the laughter
of people,

the things in your mind telling and saying
over and over again:
You are alone…

Me as a Word

Me as a word
needs no one else.
We are all we need,
for we are self-sufficient.

Me as a person
needs the contact of a
body to help hold the
place of thought into
reality…

Life

Can you find a sample of life?
If so, then hold it in your hand,
Touch it,
Smell it,
Taste it,
Does it still seem as sweet?

Can you find a sample of love?
If so, then hold it in your heart,
Feel it,
Try it,
Test it,
Does it still seem so real?

If you find these samples as sweet, as real,
then hold on,
for if not,
then it's all only a dream…

Look Towards

Look towards the earth
and you can see my warmth.

Look towards the sun
and you can see my smile.

Look towards the moon
and you can see my glow.

Look towards the stars
and you can see my happiness.

Fallen Dove

Watch out for the fallen dove,
for she will return
once again to take her place
in the world.

No one thing can keep her down.
She will rise again,
better than ever and more
intact, so watch out
for the fallen dove…

Forget Me Not

Forget me not,
for all the troubled times we had,
for all the wonderful times we shared.

Forget me not,
for the love I have for you,
for the feeling that I leave behind with you.

Forget me not,
for the memories I leave
are few…

In My Own Way

In my own way,
I like to say goodbye,
not verbally but with my action.

In my own way,
I have to say so long,
not verbally but with my action.

In my own way,
goodbye is a word that
ends or stops, it never goes on.

So in my own way,
let me, by my action, say these
words, to show you that
I care and I won't stop caring.

In my own way,
let my action speak louder or better
then words, so there can be no ending.
Let me do this in my own way…

I Am Faith

Faith, I am,
and Faith I'll always be,
for no one can take that
pleasure from me.

For Faith I am now,
and will always be. From now
until eternity.

PART II

Key of Love

Key of Love

Collections of a Fallen Dove

Faith Alanna Richardson

January 19, 1978

"This week, I guess I was in a rut. My head was totally empty.
But getting away for those four days really helped me get my act together.
I guess all I needed was to be able to think to myself, alone."

– *Faith Alanna Richardson*

The Fool

Been fooled again,
but that's okay,
just part of learning,
part of life.

Been hurt again,
but that's fine,
just part of learning,
part of life.

Oh, yes, I can handle it.
Chalk it up to growth –
'cause just part of learning,
part of life.

Footsteps of Love

Let us first walk in the
path of Friendship,
for this is a start…

And if Love follows
our footsteps, then
let it come…

And we shall welcome it,
only because Love
caught up and found us…

Say Love

'Tis the way we look at
each other,
that makes it say love.

'Tis the way we smile and play
with each other,
that makes it say love.

'Tis the way we hold and touch
each other,
that makes it say love.

'Tis the way we feel
towards one another when we're together,
that makes it say love.

'Tis all the little things we
do for one another,
that makes it say love.

Lost in Thought

Lost in thought,
not in body or Soul…

For it is thinking of
You that has me lost…

Lost in thought with
the hopes of finding

You…

Heart of Glass

When we met,
there was so much I wanted
to say, but nervousness
overcame me.

And I didn't know what
to say, or how to say what
I wanted to…

But you
are gone now, and
I'm glad I had the chance to
see, to gaze into your eyes…

If you, perhaps, were aware,
you could have looked through my coolness and calmness
and seen right through my heart,
for it is a
Heart of glass, and
so easy to break.

One Blue Rose

I once Found one Blue Rose,
It was standing in the midst
of a crowd, but somehow it
stood out.

I once Saw one Blue Rose,
and as I sat to watch it,
I noticed how beautiful it was,
shining, glowing as the Sunlight
hit its soft face.

I once Captured that one Blue Rose.
Not to be selfish – 'cause I knew
it was special and needed love and affection.

So I kept it.

It's one of a kind and happens only once to find
One Blue Rose…

To Pay the Price

One never knows the Price
one pays for Love,
nor the debt it holds.

For many times we can't
afford to repay what we gave…

And the ones who can't are marked for life,
for they will never survive.

The Price for Love is
much too high and the
loss much too great to bear…

Once Again

Once again
I tried and failed to find a Love all to myself…

Again
I've been beaten out of a chance at life's happiness.

Again
Alone and lost without the comfort of Love.

Once again
I find myself asking:

When will it be my turn?
Can I hold on, when once again I am alone…?

Alone Again

Alone again
Without someone to answer my call…

Again alone, all by myself
Without someone to care…

Again alone,
With only a shadow to keep me secure.

Again alone
Without the warmth of Love to save me from the cold.

Alone again
For no other reason, except…
It is what I want.

Lovers Twine

Lovers' Twine
is a winding love that never goes
on forever.

For once you've winded and twisted
together, you begin to choke.
Then you must let go.

For a lovers' twine is a deadly twine
that ascends upon and smothers two
closely united ones…

Out of Need

You came to me out of need.
At first I turned away,
but you, being you,
came back once more.

I opened up to let my
hesitation and fears escape
and you, being you,
said you'll wait.

Reborn again, filled
with life, I opened up to let you in.
"Trust me," I heard you say, and you, being you,
indeed I do.

You came to me out of need.
I took the chance
and Loved again…

Being Alone/Being Together

Being alone,
all by myself, is fine, 'cause
I need time to think
and just be me.

Being together
with someone special, someone you
Love, is magic. Words alone can't
describe this feeling.

Being alone/being together.
Both are wanted, both are needed,
'cause sometimes we all need that little balance
to help us deal with reality…

Sunshine

The sun need not shine when you are around.

One can recognize the beauty
not in looks, but in personality.

One can recognize the tenderness
not in touch, but by the softness of the Soul.

One can recognize these things
not from the outside alone, but also from the inside.

You are recognized for these things…

Only Briefly

You only entered into my life again,
only briefly…

You stayed only a second,
but long enough to bring back
old memories of hopes,
dreams, and fantasy…

You reentered my life
only to leave me once again.
That feeling was laid to rest
deep inside.

You came back once again,
but only briefly…

The Letter

I sent a letter to my Love
and I post-marked it "heavy."
'Cause my love is far away,
I had to tell of all the things I
truly felt.

I sent this letter,
'cause you had my heart and didn't know it
and now I need to know how you feel.

I sent a letter to my Love
many miles away, and post-
marked it, "Please Answer…"

Silent Song

The silent song
has no words, knows no key,
but has meaning full of life…

The silent song
is sung alone, by itself, for it
runs deep into the Soul…

The silent song,
a precious song, a quiet song,
sung only in the
Key of Love…

Woman

I am meek, I am strong,
I am wonderful, I am wrong.
I am happy, I am sad,

I am everything you can think of…

I am your friend, I am your sister,
I am your aunt, I am your niece,
I am your grandma, I am your mother.

Who am I? I am Woman.
The greatest thing of all.

Disengage

Disengage from life, but
not from one another.

Disengage to be free, to let go,
but not to be alone.

Disengage to reach your dreams and fantasy,
but never far from being able to grab ahold again.

Disengage only for the time needed to be you,
but only, then, until you become one again.

Goodbye

Once I learned to say Hello.
Now I must learn to say goodbye…

For me, goodbye is hard,
for it lingers on forever…

Yet, it still must be said.
And I can say it, if only you
will remember that you
meant the world to me…

And even though our worlds must grow apart,
I will never forget you.

Goodbye…

To Love Again

Love is given in only a small amount of time
and is taken while our hearts are still full.

What we do find: the comfort
to ease an aching heart,
to fill the loneliness that was left behind.

Then, like taking a pill, we search
to replace what was taken – to stop the pain.
But we find no relief, for we're still trying
To find what we had before.

We finally give up, so we ask God to spare
us the pain and send you back this way.

Our prayers go unanswered and we vow
never to Love again. We live in the shadow
of Love, haunted by the fears, the risk.

Then slowly something happens, and we begin
to live again.
What we discover is what we should have known all along:
We will survive and love again.

www.ingramcontent.com/pod-product-compliance
Lightning Source LLC
Chambersburg PA
CBHW051336120626
46547CB00016B/2569